Veil and Burn

Veil and Burn

Poems by
Laurie Clements Lambeth

University of Illinois Press

Urbana and Chicago

Manufactured in the United States of America
1 2 3 4 5 C P 5 4 3 2 1
∞ This book is printed on acid-free paper.

Library of Congress Cataloging-in-Publication Data
Lambeth, Laurie Clements
Veil and burn : poems / by Laurie Clements Lambeth.
p.   cm. — (The national poetry series)
ISBN-13: 978-0-252-03276-9 (cloth : acid-free paper)
ISBN-10: 0-252-03276-4 (cloth : acid-free paper)
ISBN-13: 978-0-252-07503-2 (pbk. : acid-free paper)
ISBN-10: 0-252-07503-X (pbk. : acid free paper)
I. Title.
PS3612.A54673V45   2008
811'.6—dc22   2007030321

The National Poetry Series

The National Poetry Series was established in 1978 to ensure the publication of five poetry books annually through participating publishers. Publication is funded by Stephen Graham, the International Institute of Modern Letters, the Joyce and Seward Johnson Foundation, the Juliet Lea Hillman Simonds Foundation, the Tiny Tiger Foundation, and Charles B. Wright III. This project is also sponsored by the National Endowment for the Arts, which believes that a great nation deserves great art.

2006 Competition Winners

Laynie Browne of Oakland, California, *The Scented Fox*
Chosen by Alice Notley, published by Wave Books

Noah Eli Gordon of Denver, Colorado, *Novel Pictorial Noise*
Chosen by John Ashbery, published by HarperCollins

Laurie Clements Lambeth of Houston, Texas, *Veil and Burn*
Chosen by Maxine Kumin, published by the University of Illinois Press

Martha Ronk of Los Angeles, California, *Vertigo*
Chosen by C. D. Wright, published by Coffee House Press

William Stobb of La Crosse, Wisconsin, *Nervous Systems*
Chosen by August Kleinzahler, published by Penguin Books

Acknowledgments

Grateful acknowledgment is made to the editors of the following publications in whose pages some of these poems originally appeared: *Alaska Quarterly Review:* "Large Loop Excision of the Temporal Zone" (originally titled "The Deeper Focus"); *American Letters and Commentary:* "Retrobulbar"; *The Bark:* "After Cancer: Dog on Her Side, Post-Amputation"; *The Cream City Review:* "What Holds"; *Disability Studies Quarterly:* "Case History: Frankenstein's Lesions"; *Gulf Coast:* "The Merle"; *Indiana Review:* "Hypoesthesia"; *The Iowa Review:* "Mesh Fragment," "Fragment Behind the Eyelid," "Needle Fragment," "Preserved Fragment," "Mosaic Fragment," "Chipped Fragment," "Fragment Dissected and Sewn," and "Brain Fragment (as Seen on a Monitor)" (all appearing in a different form); *Isotope:* "Back Lot Field Notes"; *Mid-American Review:* "In a Field Distractions Rise" and "Gingham Fragment" (originally appearing in a different form); *Nimrod International Journal:* "Dressage, or the Attempt at Training the Course of Illness," "The Spaces Between," and "Washing Up"; *The Paris Review:* "The Shaking"; and *Pebble Lake Review:* "Coming Down," "Symptoms," and "After Eight Years."

I am also grateful to Inprint, Inc. and the Houston Arts Alliance, whose support made the completion of this book possible. My tremendous gratitude to all my teachers, especially Mark Doty, for his generous reading and encouragement. I also thank Tracy Jo Barnwell, Barbara Duffey, James Allen Hall, Melanie Jordan, Miho Nonaka, Andrea Tinnemeyer, David Ray Vance, and Sasha West for their enthusiasm and patient help with drafts of this book and individual poems. Finally, my deep and abiding gratitude to my parents and my husband, Ian, who have always given me the space to write.

for Ian

She was moving far behind
the others, absorbed, like someone who will soon
have to sing before a large assembly;
upon her eyes, which were radiant with joy,
light played as on the surface of a pool.

—Rainer Maria Rilke, translated by Stephen Mitchell

Contents

Coming Down

Starting from the top, my husband undoes
   nineteen nub buttons lining my spine.

Three open. *Where exactly is the flaw that brought down*
   the price? He's searching for tears in stitching.

Plucking the side of the skirt, I show him:
   faint streaks of yellow flowing from the bodice,

seeping dark into the skirt's organza folds,
   each widening down to wash. Six. A kiss.

An hour of worry at I Do, I Do, for naught.
   All white yellows over time, I say.

Nine: I can feel half my back undone.
   This dress just aged a little faster, oxidized

and burned in the shop window . . . happens to silk.
   Nineteen. He opens me, guides the straps

down my arms. All that fabric purling
   at my legs, foam and waves taller than my knee—

for a moment I feel the birth of Venus. Then
   I see my body: bulges smoothed by corset, spine

stippled with lesions, glowing red injection
   lumps studding my thighs. I hide them well,

most of the time. His hands stroke them, hold their heat,
   subcutaneous Interferon half-globes.

In the mirror I wear a luminous necklace.
   I see him looking down my body to the gown.

He offers his hand to help. —*For now I can
   manage.* Still in my pumps, I hoist the right leg

out of its silk encasement, stretch heel to floor.
   A moment for balance. Raise the left high

over folds, boundless yards of yellowed cream.
   Like climbing off a horse, I say. One boot in stirrup,

the other hanging at its side—from such height
   you let go and eventually reach ground.

Symptoms

It seems to have a predilection for females.

—on MS, from *Multiple Sclerosis: A Guide for Patients and Their Families*

I'll try to tell you how it feels: girdle
my grandmother wore, tight-laced corset
worn by her mother in Wales, but it seldom slips
from my ribcage. No hooks or laces, only

spaces of remission, then relapse,
a trip to the ancient clothes again:
crinolines, skirts grazing ankles, long
satin embroidered sleeves that rub and pull

naked skin, saying, *now and then you must
try to feel through this, and this.* All that fabric
wound around torso, legs, the dresses
and sheets binding to keep me in

bed. *The cure is rest,* they tell me. Dizzy,
drunk when I haven't drunk, I'm drawn
to the wall to prop me. I've been known to sport
a cane, per the fashion, to smooth the gait.

Fix my mouth in a loose pout when speech
eludes its muscles, tired, stiff as the garments
that hold me. On occasion, they'll fall
to reveal this body, a window of cellophane

wrapping my limbs, a ring for each finger.

The Spaces Between

In memory of R. L. Crosby,
Horse-trainer 1927–1999

In the photo I've never seen, she stands (or leans),
bowlegged as Richard beside her, his legs
   long, slim, still roundly gripped
to the sides of some young thoroughbred

   visible only in the space between

his knees. Her legs, hind and front, curl
outward at the knee and hock, inward
   down to fetlock and ergot joints,
the long cannon and shank bones bent
   to accommodate the arc of age,

     a language we can see, not speak,

      an alphabet of limbs.

•

This mare's movement forms a sentence,
unintelligible. Unable to speak last requests. *What*
   is it that you want? I daub
her bedsores with scarlet oil; the sting
  evident in flinches,
         failed attempts to kick me.

She's gone down again, scraped her sides
   all night on the stall floor. I mark
each wound on the eye, legs, pelvis with red
circles of balmy correction: *don't try lying down again, or else.*

•

When she casts herself down in the stall one can hear her
           become the barn, shifting loudly.
Her head beats the wall. Legs, letters flying through air.
The sentence cast
              down to where it wants to be, throwing

                          now and *now* into the night.

•

        The next day, Richard walks me to the barn. I know
he's been in for chemo but I say nothing: a moment
      when there is too much space
               for articulation of my fear, his pain.

                I point out measured red spots in the dirt. *How . . .?*
           His vocal chords spotted with lesions,
       he whispers, *sometimes these guys have to drag*
the horses to get them into the truck, or could be
      a hole between the trailer's slats.

        I look at him and desire what I cannot have:
               all I love compressed, no spaces, no end,
those legs to hold a horse between them always. His gaze
               answers: *At some point an animal must*

                  give in to the sentence given.

                What I didn't see until then:
the loaded truck that came to hoist the mare's body, the barn
           cats rolling in the dark pool the needle left,
the even spots of blood trailing

              across the ground, ellipses.

Murky sheen of horse eyes. How they roll. First appaloosa I ever saw frightened me with the whites of its eyes, reversals of its spots. The position of the orbits allows the horse to see to the side, but forces the mind to fill in the space directly in front. Blinders: all a race or carriage horse sees fits a narrow field of haze. It moves forward, as always.

My grey gelding lacked pigment in his inner eyelid, needed protection. To block UV rays, we looped a plush-lined, mesh fly mask over his ears, velcroed it under the cheek. The plastic grid before his eyes dissolved to shade in proximity.

The optometrist handed me a black plastic disk on a handle, hundreds of holes punched through. This to cut glare. To train. I pulled it close to my eye, imagined myself carrying around this reverse monocle. Pince-nez? I'd rather wear the fly mask, go to pasture.

In a Field
Distractions Rise

Too much marveling at the electricity of blue
   dragonflies and screens of gnats in their hover
      to notice the dark ducks rising from the lake;

too filled with voice calling the dog back
   from her bounds after wingflaps in flight
      to comprehend the machine of those paws parting,

hear the skein of geese on their opposing air path
   or the feather-water and dog-pant whir
      as the ducks descend and the dog returns,

affectionate but of a thrill beyond you—;
   when the egret unfolds its white-flame
      wings and leaps its frame to reedy solitude

on the lake's opposite shore, it replaces all speech
   with thick tuck and space, wings collapsing to the breast.
      The dog steps up to her belly in water. You know

what she's after—that white and shining figure—
   because it's your wish, too: who wouldn't want to
      embrace that bird like air, feel its bones shift to leave you?

First pain of optic neuritis digs behind the eye, grates against movement: a constellation of tiny cobalt lights on the right eyelid's interior. In bed I consciously positioned my eye to brace against pressure when it rolled to the side, or against the pillow. The eye in place, I watched the blue stars dance for me. I missed them when they stopped appearing. Their absence marked the cusp of the next unknown phase, and I wondered if this was my last dazzling thing.

Riches

O body swayed to music, O brightening glance,
—W. B. Yeats

Stamped, we enter Rich's. The club
   thick with buzz, hum—
         sonic palms on each
     close shoulder. A string of blue
beads at my feet, swept
        to the edge—I lift it
up to my hair, veil
my eyes with blue under black light.
    More beads
  and feathers, leather,
     suits (three-pieced and one)—
    sequins and haloes:
         I LOVE YOU rings
  a man's head, L.E.D. red's
travel, flash, dazzle
   in the midst of motion.

Upon the pulses, breath
  shared in clouds above,
all these men hold light
  sticks in their mouths, neon
beacons on wrists;

they float and sway
and shiver together
and she and I
here because there is safety
for women.
No offers of drinks, no
fingers roamed,
not for us, at least.
We hold
hands, reach
the floor, wiggle to a music
we do not call our own,
two women
flinging bodies
in this air, this glow,
this space of no space.

No time, only movement
and returning eternal
echoes of drum and bass.
We feel our bodies
but lose distinction
between other dancers and ourselves:
Stray elbows and hips
become extensions of our own,
aftershave and sweat, ours.
And he, from behind, lays a steady
palm on her shoulder, then
mine. *You are such a cute*
couple—both

so beautiful, he says
    above music. *Where are you*
from? How did you meet? We thank
  the man, talk some.
        We do not say
     we are no couple; —tonight
       the cloud above us
            crystallizes a shower of jewels.
He makes us one
   in the air
         of all our breathing.
    Praise to all flinging bodies—
    This music, our buoy, contains us.

Is blindness darkness, blur, whirl of ether? Do you remember pretending to be blind? Closing your eyes, counting steps from bedroom to bathroom, feeling your way along a wall? I've been practicing. If I say I can do my hair with my eyes closed, that might testify to its messiness, but what would it matter if I couldn't see it? What good's a mirror? Let it contain clouds.

Seizure,
or Seduction
of Persephone

I convulsed so   hard I broke
open, broke   the earth,
erupted and   pushed out
a narcissus   by the roots.

It doesn't   matter where
the flower   broke on my body,
through the   skin, a pimple,
my head, or   the belly.

I could not   tell you.
What I can   say is this:
my limbs   flailed and seized
in the bed.   I watched, both

inside and   outside, skin
the sheet   of a Richter scale,
delicate   needles charting
the shifting   of earth's plates,

limbs all   speaking
unknown   tongues, plotting
maps and   pathways deep
into the   body. As he held

me still   in that bed,
how was   I to discern
if he then   learned
his way   through the flesh

into my   need, or if
he chose   this blue moment
to come   out, rupture
the field   from within

my own   unruly body?
Seduction: nothing but
a man's hand   depressing
and a flower   jolting out.

Some void   here between my hips.

Swirl the medication with saline, draw it up into the syringe
through the blue micro pin. Flick the syringe with finger or pen
to release any bubbles back into the vial. Unscrew the micro
pin from the syringe and twist on the 23-gauge needle. It's long,
as far as needles go: darts through approximately $1^{1}/_{4}$ inches of
flesh. Known to cleave muscle fibers. At these times the muscle
jumps involuntarily. Measure a space to inject: one hand at the
tip of patella, the other where the leg and hip join. In this square,
between these moles. With thumbnail, mark the point to be
injected. Dig. Sweep alcohol swab over the target.

One holds the syringe like a pen: thumb and forefinger. However,
if one breaks through the page with a pen, it's a mistake.
Throughness is the goal of the needle.

The hand may stop the needle short of skin up to seven times
before contact. It gleams cleanly above the thigh.

I wonder what the needle sees on its descent.

Large Loop
Excision of the
Temporal Zone

for Georgia O'Keeffe

Pale red and smooth, a little mouth inside.
A flower. Red Amaryllis, each fold
deep crimson at center. Brush strokes push out,
drag pigment up each minute crease of inner
corolla. Georgia, the clinic shows me

my insides on a video monitor,
aided by microscopic vision,
studio lighting. How could you know
so long ago, without your own speculum
or microscope, what lay deepest inside

a woman: tissue, mouth, amaryllis?
You saw *something unexplored about women*
that only a woman can explore,
painted it a lush metaphor. Today
I witness the tenor to your vehicle,

directed by the surgeon, interns, nurses,
my closest friend's fingers wrapping mine.
Now she's seen more of me than any man
I've loved. We watch them anaesthetize
the cervix, four shots, extreme close-up to fill

the screen above the action, larger
than life but alive. A thin string of fluid
probes out the center; there is no etiquette
here. You might call it natural, *vulgar*
but magnificent, this spit. Like a stamen

in your Red Amaryllis, filaments
drooping and surging upward, tipped with gold
anthers, liquid motion from a center,
pistil or tight mouth exposed on canvas,
on screen. It is swabbed with a vinegar wash

to illuminate abnormality—
what must be removed before it can grow
into cancer. The cervix transforms, turns blue
as sky through bones in the desert. A pocket
within a pelvis, but mine encased by flesh.

A wash of iodine strokes corrections
on this sky, makes flesh more akin to flora—
corolla and pistil, a heavy pigment.
And they go in, hum of electric charge
powering the wire loop chosen to excise

the lesion. We view it on screen, slicing
off the abnormal, feel minutely shocked,
relieved. The instrument pulls up a wake
of pigment, a flood of red, swirling.
This once I try to turn my head away

from the image. My friend squeezes my hand
for strength to face the action on screen. Feeling
no pain, I pretend this blood is your paint,
watch the final act. A smaller loop, yellow-
handled, undoes the center, that neat, tight

mouth. One round sweep and it's gone, newly
misshapen, wide hole inside a hole. The last
coat comes to stop the bleeding: Monsel's
Solution applied with swabs. Burnt sienna
brushed up a wake of crimson: ochre,

a flower once more. Relief and wonder.
The center, oddly black, suggests both
utter possibility and the grotesque.
Georgia, you'd understand—presence in loss,
what is taken: what was saved. What remains:

your giant Poppy on screen and within me,
a bloom of color overcome by something
deeper, the wide, black center, a cavern
offering from its depths a jewel: a jade
half-globe stamen lit from its underbelly.

Frantic human shape, pressed through a door. Then, tree,
water, sky. I wept to see it again, with my new framed vision.
"La Perspective Amoureuse": Magritte. I claim this bursting
through the solid world: haloed brightness at the center of field.
Almost pretend the bright, diffused middle is the strength to defy
physics, arrange landscape.

Onion

This morning, when your hand traced
the skin on my collarbone and throat
I could smell the onion you had chopped
last night in the pores of your fingers.

With each pass of your hand the repeated
scent, warm, delicious, grew as familiar
as the sensation of your particular touch,
as the windows' wide shafts slanting to wake us.

Cutting Distance

for Ian

*Clumsy, they fumble for hands in their first
dance, he reaching for her left, she, offering*

*her right. They laugh. She finally holds up
the left, apologizes for leading.* Oh, I wouldn't

know, *he says. His hand glides over hers,
an orchid closing, drinking each small knuckle.*

This is when she knew, and they drew closer.
Somehow things seem pretty, ideal even, set

in third person. Like I'm watching it in a mirror of
a mirror, the fixing of all the flaws singular

reflection causes, the final gesture of our hands'
glide more graceful, deliberate, like a flower

in the night closing in on what it holds. *She, held,
unafraid.* More certain, diffused, than if I were

to admit my part in all of it. What is it,
mystery, reserve? All it accomplishes is distance.

When the song stopped it was you and I who kissed,
you and I who closed in on each other like petals,

straining as orchids do in time-lapsed photography,
trembling their stretch to hold on. Metaphor (like this)

amazes me, too, the way it distances but brings close
the lie and the truth, the actor and the role. Truth

be told, you stole fractions of me when we parted,
when the dawn rose and we couldn't stay closer

than the image, the petals peeling us open, the glass
telling us who we are. No pretense. No mystery.

No extra mirror. Only a single view. And then
your marks on my skin: chin rashing red, lips

blooming a field of blisters now turned to scars.
How I miss those red pillows pulled up by your kisses.

But I live with their marks, marked, I'd like to think,
by fate or something greater: mistake—your right hand,

my lead. Metaphor transcends language. You and I,
we transcend the figurative. We cut the distance like a stem.

People "in my condition" lose vision gradually, sometimes without noticing. I want to notice, if it happens. I close each eye periodically to monitor change. Are objects darker through the right eye than through left, or does it only seem that way? Does a bright rim surround the perimeter of my vision through that right eye, or is perception disoriented from some other source (worry, fear of blindness, some lesion on a neural pathway in the occipital lobe)? Periphery: partially eclipsed, clouded.

One eye closed, objects not only move a considerable distance, but lighten or darken with particles, shadow mixed with light. Parallax, a game from childhood: I'd allow the right eye to brandish dominance over the left, unfocused. Growing up with "a wandering eye," my left one bobbling on a loose tether, I let its pupil float to the far corner, though I could easily call it over to play. I could wipe a person from my view and bring him back by letting one eye take over. Now I wonder, the right eye struggling to focus, what the left recorded all those times I granted the right one the privilege of framing.

After Eight Years

What ardor
led you to break
your mouth from mine,
thumb on my jaw,
and stare, mired
in the thrill of it,
before diving back?
I read
        the words
insist and *collapse*.
Flashed
on your eyes:
every other time
you held that
strange intensity
back to the first,
                stacked
in palimpsest, or
spliced like frames
of a celluloid—
no, nitrate reel:
a movie of that
pulsing gaze
directed
        straight out
the screen. I learned

once that nitrate
decomposes
and ignites, fueled
by its own bright
oxygen. If
that's true,
          then how
are we preserved?
When you looked at me
I embraced it
but wondered (marveled)
at its source; asked
myself, *What is this*
he's looking at?

In Japan,
Woman Can Doze
with Man Pillow

Associated Press,
September 30, 2004

It keeps holding me all the way
through the night on its stuffed arm.
This pillow does not betray.

I know this one will always stay
here beside me, palm to plumper palm.
I like to sleep holding someone's hand, the way

I did with men who'd leave by light of day,
even my husband, now gone, who'd toss and squirm
as I dozed. *This pillow does not betray.*

No head or legs, but enough to lay
my head on, and *at my side there's always something warm.*
It keeps still, soft, *holding me all the way*

until I wake. How much would you pay
to feel mildly comforted, safe and calm?
No worry of breath or heartbeat to *betray*

permanence, no flesh to wrinkle and decay.
The manufacturer said, *Nothing better pillow than human form.*
Guaranteed to *hold* its shape around *me all the way*
until I leave, worn with tears, the form I *betray.*

Work

Your barn gloves lay folded, like hands
on a prayer book, over throw pillows
by the bedside. Rumpled and worn
at the knuckles, the dark spots shade them
enough, like magic or art, to fool me
into thinking your hands fill the gloves.
They reach, maybe touch something—
a pitchfork, a rake, my ribs.
Or flakes of hay. Why not? Alfalfa
still clings to those gloves, even when
you're not here. And your shoes, upturned
under the bed (though you've been gone a week)
lift their horse-urine stench
through the mattress. Each night they lead me—
shoes and gloves, urine and hay—
to you, to our work under rafters:
cleaning paddocks and box stalls,
sifting manure from fresh bedding.
No better work than this.

Dorothy awakens to Aunt Em by her side, pressing a folded cloth to the girl's forehead. She's been knocked unconscious. Judy Garland's huge eyes examine with confusion her Uncle Henry's farm hands. "And you were there, and you . . ." What line dare divide dream from memory? Something like the gingham check of Dorothy's dress: lines bisecting each other, dissolving to minuscule dots upon close inspection: porous perimeter through which things come and go, and are lost.

Into Wind

The Nerves sit ceremonious, like Tombs
—Emily Dickinson

but the child dreams of running away, up
the asphalt grade from beach to home,
the zone away from the tidal wave,

                  and it is always

a tidal wave that follows her in this
dream, and though she has won track and field
events in this small town, now she plunges each

                  foot to the ground

unsteadily, more a trudge than a sprint,
more like walking into wind. There is a force
pressing back against each leg, something thick

                  saying, *no*

and *no*. Turning, she eyes the green height
over her shoulder. She looks to her legs
that plod like ancient wax seals on letters

                  she will never send,

not in this horror, in this dream. Where
to place blame or cause? There is no one but
the child and her swimsuit full of sand

                  squishing wrongly.

Perhaps this is what holds her back. She scoops
chunks from the back and crotch, but this detains.
Why do we waste so much time assigning

                  cause, blame?

Years later, she can't help herself from reading
the dream as one would read omens, calling
back the feeling of true slowness
                                        now afloat in her body,

legs pushing weakly against unseen winds.
The nerves are one cause, but to address them
formally does not erase the symptoms
                                        they produce:

the stiff calves, the heavy air, the inching push
and push. Is *the hour of lead* a slow re-
lapse? A fall backward, into memory,
                                        into dream, a first

cause for illness, something prophetic
we can point to, say, *this is it. Amputate!*
Why search at all? The wave will come, or
                                        the child will wake.

The body will remember what it will
of the dream, stitch and stow it there
until air thickens, steps slow—*a wooden way*
                                        regardless grown.

Ode to the Upper Lip

O delicate and subtle row,
o lines that grow downward,
spiny fence stakes every one,
forgive me your uprooting,
o moustache:
equivalent to an adolescent boy's
tender growth, fuzz
too rampant for beauty.

How else to harness you but lift and rip?

Legs and armpit receive the razor's stroke,
eyebrow and chin the tweezers' nick,
but you have known the burn
of depilatories and bleach,
the repeated twang of Persian thread,
tight fiber rolling over unready hairs,
twisting them up by the roots.
Dissolved, camouflaged, cut,
yanked, tweezed in a desperate hour,
exhumed, weeded, mown.
O how you suffer. Unwelcome, you return.

Irena coats half of you in green goo.
You let me know the temperature?
she says. Blink once for yes, warm,
for a moment soothing.

A cooled edge teased up by steel,
quick spring of motion, and you,
naïve hairs, now inhabit wax.

With her wand, wide wooden spatula,
Irena waves a mysterious circle
over what remains of you.
Stray strings of wax
rise in air and quiver.
Last rip. Kleenex and pressure.

O moustache, if it were the fashion,
I would cultivate and twist your ends,
eager to see (and feel!) how long
you'd grow, how you'd curl.
But now I must deny you.
Irena hands me the mirror.

A little red now, but . . . you know,
she says, smoothing on a lavender
shimmer, *beauty hurts*.

Case History: Frankenstein's Lesions

When the great doctor's assistant—Fritz
or Igor, some hunchbacked henchman—beheld
the row of preserved brains afloat in glass,
did he pause to consider the irony

of such delicacy housed by potential harm
before he let drop the jar marked "Genius"?
First the shatter, then the spill, then the plop

rather like a peeled orange dropped and opening
a little, swirl of corpus callosum stretched
between tilted hemispheres. Panic,
then he picked another: not the abnormal

brain of a murderer, frontal lobe dented
with insufficient fissures (as Whale filmed),
but what he read as "Abby Normal,"

a brain atrophied, mottled with grey lesions
visible only when sliced in the autopsy theatre.
Mine was the one jar that did not break,
and I sloshed against its walls with each lurch

of the hunchback's pitching, tilting ramble.
Nobody sliced me; I was too precious
whole, tight bundle of tissue disembodied,

"just resting, waiting for a new life to come,"
said Dr. F. He didn't know how much I'd like
to rest, stay out of bodies for a while.
Alas, now I work this body

as best I can. The monster (how I hate
what they call us, but I suppose it's true)
presented no symptoms at first, capable

of strength to match his proportions,
performing feats of violence when provoked
in his chamber. It was all going so *well,*
I nearly forgot about our illness. Then

he began dribbling his trouser fronts (too
humiliating for me to acknowledge
personally) and we took a while

to recall the simplest words: "fire" fell
to nothing, then, "f . . . , f . . . , f . . . , fancy? fast?"
Which made Fritz think we liked the torch's dance.
Torture. We did away with him, yes, but

perhaps I just didn't know our own strength.
It took some getting used to, as I had
formerly inhabited the cranium

of a cripple who willed her corpse to science.
Just when things began working smoothly, brain
and body as one, the body began
to cave to the ills I had brought it.

The legs moved less freely. Our feet felt heavy,
as though they wore sixty-pound boots. I hear
that was Karloff's trick to imitate our gait.

That man got it right, a very good likeness,
probably because he more than anyone
comprehended the absolute effort
needed to heave one foot forward, and the next.

Laughing villagers toddled along roadsides,
saying we walked like a duck. Echoes
of the cripple's life. Quacks, taunts. No duck,

but a monster too weak to chase them down.
Torso before feet, we shook only the earth,
tipping into the woods. Left Arm, pale hand
stitched to deep brown wrist, tried to pull a limb

from a tree to use as walking stick,
but the fingers would not tighten as I
intended. Right Arm assisted, but could not

force it from the trunk. We plucked a flower, limp
hand round the bloom, not the stem. Petals and phlox
sifted through our weakened fingers
to the ground. What else to do but plod on?

We learned to lean into trees for support,
the way a drunk would lean against walls
following a night's consolation. The creatures

in the eaves fled our advance, left us alone
with our sensations, or lack of them.
All along I thought this might happen.
With grief more than horror I've greeted

each fresh apathy in our limbs. I dare
not share this with Dr. F., or my toes.
They'd be so numbly . . . disappointed.

Within me, though, I feel something changing:
not the spread of lesions, more a tremble
in my cortex, as though this broad skull
sutured shut is not enough to contain me.

When we look down to our trailing feet below,
it happens, that theremin playing
our abdomen down to trill in our legs,

and I'm close to bursting. Curse the skies that watch
us buckle, the shock of our birth night's storm
now played out from within, as L'hermitte
discovered and named. I want to say

there is no discovery, only repetition
and return. And the rage that pulses down
this monster body, frail and more fierce than fire.

Alfred Hitchcock
Meets The Blob

It's the moment in the picture
after Bergman coolly escapes,
and that monochrome pistol turns to screen.
Blown-up, tall as a monster, the image
of that mocked-up wooden hand

mechanically pulls the trigger, shifts
the barrel, and blasts the screen red,
light spraying down, image firing back.
If only now it were possible to graft
Spellbound to *The Blob*:

the Technicolor monster's ruby goo
entering, filtered, sliced
through heater vents in a blue wall
behind the projectionist who is reading,
unsuspecting any spectacle

outside the words in his bent paperback.
Silent, the creature divides and unifies
the body with a constant drive
that is to be admired. As it rises
to devour the man, and only then,

it blocks the screen black, melting
the painted frames of gunfire
with its body's thicker mass.
And what does our projectionist think,
as the audience goes restless

and he faces his last moments?
Jell-O? Cranberry relish? Pulp novel come true?
When the blob spreads its shining heft
to the seats below, do they scream
because they have to turn around?

In Hollywood's golden age, the camera was often veiled by a thin piece of fabric to dissolve any harsh features or wrinkles in close-ups. The cameraman burned cigarette holes into the fabric to bring the eyes to sparkle. I have a feeling that my vision is something between the veil and the burn, or that it alternates between the two.

After Cancer:
Dog on Her Side,
Post-Amputation

More than a year after it was done,
I'm petting what used to be
the thin gap—white strip

banked by copper fur—
between front legs,
awed at the ease of my reach.

Here I trace the incision's scar,
ridge of tissue once bulked
by bone, curled knot that burned,

hairless, like a question mark
—my touch freely passing
over that chest space grown

rampant with long hairs
to the remaining leg. Delicate
inner elbow. What was it like

to first feel a touch here,
this hidden space unblocked
by absence? Was it radiant,

an opening? Three legs left
I know will follow, as will the rest.
Not yet. O strong and sculpted

creature, how you do
find pleasure and endure.
Her head lifts: *pet more now.*

Inheritance

1.

My mother says she was holding
her mother's hand when her mother was hit
by a New York streetcar. She survived

a while, left arm and breast in pain
for months. A cyst the size of my mother's
lips pushed out her mother's breast.

Radiation, my mother says, *was primitive
in those days.* She recalls the side-effect, a burn
in the center of the chest, a deep red circle.

2.

Days before a dance, prom or homecoming,
my mother's cheeks burned. Without a mother,
she had tall lanky boys with names

like Carl LaBorie, Jack Barringer,
Harry Peabody, Bill O'Toole, who liked
her strapless and full-skirted, cheeks

pinched and flushed, lips blooming red.
They brought carnation corsages and waited
in the marble foyer while my mother

artfully applied all those powders
to her chest, flushing red in splotches
above the bustier line of a sky-

blue prom dress. After they took her
home, she'd weep at the sight of this sign,
this giant rose blooming on her chest.

Hypoesthesia

For now (who knows how long now is) his touch is nothing but warmth
    and trace
trailing his hand up my thigh and around my stomach. I feel a little
something crystallize after each pass of his hand, then it's dust.

Whoever thought sex could be so literally senseless? The first time (*my*
    first time)
I cried a little because I did not want it, but gave to make my boyfriend
    stop asking.
That was a different kind of senselessness.

I wanted to cry this time, too, another first since the new flare-up broke:
feet, knee, thigh, stomach, hip, hollow of the back, neither my body nor
    my skin
but a loose-fitting carapace, bubble, prosthetic even.

                                        Are you touching me,
I thought to ask, but instead watched as he kissed each part and caressed
and did what we do when I feel right. I didn't say   *I can't feel that,*
but let his hands and mouth travel.

For the first time in my life I let go of my body a while and looked down
with fascination at the man I love in the process of loving me—:
the way the window's meager light managed

to illuminate his nails with each finger's lengthening, how it raised
his tendons (like spines) before his knuckles into glow. Stunning
to see his eyebrows and lashes crush, devoted,

with each kiss planted along my belly, to feel only the cool afterward.
Strange that now would be the time I comprehend our otherness, these
    bodies
wanting more: luminous, impossible whole.

On My Husband's Birthday
I Read Obituaries

Emma Phillips, Lencho Villa,
Irene Veronica Ghezzi.
Emma smiles over her shoulder
in miniature above a narrow
strip of lives, top left-hand corner.
Willa Fowler lived to 103,
outlived Clifford. No children.
Worked in Chicago
at International Harvester.
Greg Bruce from Wyoming, gone
at nearly half Willa's years.
Both Helge and Louis Nelson,
dead within a month of each other,
share one column. I imagine this
as the way we'd go, but there are
also Mr. Bruce and Mrs. Fowler—
early death and widowhood.
In the rear field the local hawk
pans the ground for breakfast.
The scrub is dry this August,
the dramas of the earth larger
than we care to know. I leave him
the half-moon of buttered raisin swirl,
and we make plans, drink more coffee,
watch the hummingbird at the well.
So fast spins the heart in that green breast.

Reluctant
Pegasus

1. *Saddle*

Always something between hide and hide,
soft pad of foam, thin cushion, blanket.
As if the sting of leather
        on horse skin would be too great
when pressed to withers, ribs,
        cinched across a heart.
                        As if it were too expansive,
        pommel, cantle, seat, flaps.
It could gall flesh with its rubbing.

                    •

Richard willed his corpse to UCLA
    when he was in hospice.

On the radio, medical students
        finish dissecting cadavers.
                    The face or hands
        are the last to be revealed,
after they've stretched the skin back,
plucked organs, held lymph nodes in hand.
                Some can't take it, to see a person
        attached to the body inspected,
    the hide stretched and pinned.

(Hands: He could lead a horse by holding
its face in his hands—one on the nasal bridge,
one stroking the cheek—whispering, *here, son.*)

(Face: When his hair fell out, he did a shuffle
in the barn, tipped his cap and bowed,
mouth set in an open grin, vaudevillian ta-dah.)

•

I am cleaning the saddle he left me.
My damp rag circles the flaps
where his knees would go.

Spinny, Admiral, Nick.
Richard reunited with his horses.

I must keep it from cracking.

2. Membrane

A foal emerges from the womb.
I stretch back the white
membrane veiling his nose.

He breathes first breaths,
his nostrils straining.

My child, I say, warming him
with my towel, feeling him
kick thin tissue off his legs.
His hooves flash their unhardened
fingers, scraping softly in straw.

I do not wash my hands
before sleep; instead,

carry the smell of birth
to my bed, wrapping myself in
the folds of thin sheets.

3. At the Wild Horse Sanctuary

Each has his partner
in the bachelor herd.

They brush sides
without kicking.

The palomino gnaws
the rump of the sorrel

who bows his head,
eyes half-closed.

The bay grinds his teeth
on the muscled arc

of shoulder where
neck meets wither,

and the roan returns it.
A quiver of pleasure.

4. In Praise of Proud Flesh

Things are easier when the heat is dry.
The geldings graze the bases of foxtails,
leaving green plants alone. I scrub algae
from their trough, large enough to bathe in.

The gray gelding comes to nudge my hip, scrape
sweat from the spaces between his ears
and forelock. I think he's trying to help me.
In the dust this is easy to imagine.

Easy to believe the illusions:
that horses desire human form,
that the dapple gray's nudge is an attempt
to scrub his way into my skin.

Easy to comprehend, in this
dry heat, that only horses and humans
grow mounds of proud flesh over their wounds,
thick spongy pads to cushion gashes, burns.

Easy to feel four-legged,
heave the weight of iron horseshoes
from water trough to pasture gate.

5. Reluctant Pegasus

My poor cane is wounded, but I'm all right;
another chip in the handle. No longer
a three-legged woman, I'm a gimp,
a limper with a numb leg, no sense
of *enjambement,* no stride, except
at the wrong moments, maybe a near
fall to scare me, or the sense of a skirt
against the skin where there is no
skirt, so it comes as no surprise
when that numb leg sprouts a tiny wing
at the ankle, another at the knee,
a fluttering one gracing the calf—

and look, up it goes, into the air,
out the window over fountains
where I find myself dancing,
doing a can-can without the right
costume, but I'm still kicking,

like a bay horse I once saw lifted
from a ravine, flailing his legs, dancing
as the helicopter raised him,
a reluctant pegasus who may have seen
the wings I see, flying on some
other volition than his own, his head

drooping from side to side, flanks writhing
toward earth, edging out of the harness
into the air, those wings failing him
as he loosened the thick stitches,
bouncing that cable holding him up . . .

I remember him floating a bit,
then his descent into the Pacific,
his legs still kicking, and I guess
that is what happens to the few
who, when given the chance, are still
reluctant (my toe's just hit water)
to fly: the bruised world attracts.

6.

Tattoos of creatures with flowering horns climb the thumb and
shoulder of the Pazyryk Ice Maiden of Siberia. Wild silk blouse,
headdress of felt. Archaeologists deduce: shaman, visionary,
prophet. Her olive skin, first thawed, nearly glowed alive, pliable,
sutured with horse hair thread, body stuffed with peat and bark.
Eyes removed in the mummification process, sockets packed with
fur. I imagine lengths of the fur extending beyond the ridge of
brow and cheekbone, two dark suns.

Preserved with her under ice, her six horses were sacrificed and
laid just outside the burial chamber to accompany the Ice Maiden
to the pasture world of the afterlife. Scientists opened their bodies.
Larva of deer flies in their stomachs: the burial took place in June.

7. Pegasus, a Ghost

August was the month for both of us to leave
California, I'm told, but you went before me,
without my knowing. You left trails
of manure behind you, dried balls that scattered

whenever I tried to look for you.
Truthfully, I forgot about you for a while.
I had to. But now and then I invented stories.
A runaway, I decided. Yes. You broke

the door of your holding cell, leaped the fence,
ran through Arizona, chestnut coat blazing back
unceasing sun. In that story it set atop
your withers, scorched your skin to black,

overheating your eyes into stars, huge
and fiery, inside-out and glowing.
I told myself it was the sun that killed you.
You died in other stories too, the times

I decided you left the west for some
new pasture, some new owner who fell in love
with your grace but not your spirit. You tore in
to his arms, his neck, kicked his breath out,

showed him what you're made of.
The morning after, he came to feed with a shotgun,
pointed straight at those teeth. You cowered.
In another, someone rode you nonstop for days

in a heavy western saddle, long-shanked iron bit,
until you heaved yourself into buck, a burst
before fatigued collapse. I know
the way the real story goes; it ends

in Texas at a slaughterhouse where the only
memory the flannel-shirted men would have
of you would be your spirit: hoof and tooth.
Unruly horse, I hope you gave them hell.

8. *To the Gray I Can No Longer Ride*

Ill again, synapses
misfiring, pulsing wild with downward
glances, like shocks, momentary lapses
from remission. Chin up, it's onward
with my cane, a slow hobble on three
legs, the left of no use right now.

Last night I watched others dance without me;
today I watch the girth sink in, plow
round your ribs. Someone else will saddle
you today while I sink low under
your stable quilt. I watch her straddle
you, your mouth turn to froth. I wonder

at how much you know: when the ride is done,
you take my cane in your teeth. You run.

9. *What Holds*

It is the ring on your finger, a promise
of jewels. Loop you make with each black
boot lace, thick knot tightened before riding.

Knuckle hole worn by your left index
finger in the crocheted riding glove.
Wide arc of a toothed curry comb

returning up the dappled shoulder, against
the nap of fur. It can be found in the short girth
buckled across the horse's heart, bit rings,

the round-ring jointed snaffle, chomped at,
so soon. The band across a white blazed
nose, another that latches under

the throat. The shape of rein, loosened
then pulled taut. Weedy arena
you ride, circle of poles and mesh.

It is the murky eye of the horse,
the tight circles to contain him, inside
the larger ring, training by diameter.

It is also the serpentine used to fool
him into thinking he's going somewhere.
Minuscule bubbles of sweat settling

onto fur, the nostril, and the breath
released in clouds. The repeated path
of the buzzard above you, searching

scrub. It is the downed pole the horse jumps
to free himself of the arena,
of you. It can be seen in the arc of each

swift kick to the air, in the broken
ring of horseshoe flashed before you.
That broken ring is what can stop a heart.

10. *Dressage, or The Attempt at Training*
    the Course of Illness

  The numbness migrates,
      charts the slowest route from left foot to my ribcage
    along the thigh grown accustomed
   to gripping a horse's abdomen, squeezing cues of forward,
reverse, *passage*, side-pass right. This numbness presses in, might be
    a cue to *me* (*cue* so close to *cure*) to move
      or lie down, lord knows which. Maybe this pressure, both
over and under
     sensation, could become the thin bristles
      —needles and pins is such an inadequate phrase—
    of sorrel hair against the skin, soft, yet
       irritating, a muscular wall of motion in the space
   where nothing touches at all.
          Further north, the journey traces
     paths along my waist, midsection, settles there, the manifestation
    this disease takes as it pleases, imprinting my body by stripping
away sensation and offering something else.
          Or perhaps I am the horse,
   this numbness squeezing my waist like a leather three-buckle girth,
  like legs. Or—I can make it better: a lover's hands there and there

on my body, holding me so that when I graze
my own hand across my stomach I see him feelingly, the subdued
sensation of someone else's skin pressed against my own,
the feeling of someone there, but not there.
Look, on my stomach,
Look, if you can, at the invisible colonists finding home in my neurons.
How they tear myelin, how they eat of my flesh, invite
me to make metaphors for this disease, to comfort, but
I'm sick of it. This is when I pull the reins.

Muted shades in cells of varying sizes suggest a numeral or pathway. Ishihara Plates Test, a book open on my lap. This to detect deficiency in the perception of color. *Facets, panes of colored glass, parcels of land, as seen from a great height, a map that goes nowhere. Fragments, divisions. Museum lighting burns my eye.* The nurse instructs me to trace my finger over the path, left to right. *At the time of painting, Paul Klee was in his second year with scleroderma, the skin of his fingers growing taut, hard, numb.* She turns the page, points. Another path. *Across the painting, arrows rise and stumble direction through an approximation of center. This, the way to the citadel.* Another page, so subtle I half-guess as I trace my finger. *The arrows end at no destination in particular. The citadel is either impenetrable, or it is nothing.* I think of the other people who have dragged their fingers across these wavy distinctions, where their paths led. *I am convinced the painting's pathway leads out of the picture.*

Wrong Turn
Near Pecos

I don't know where I am.
The road's inhabitants don't know
what I am. Tentative, reserved,

they hop onto asphalt, until all
the jackrabbits, thirty-one, freeze,
held by high beams. The asphalt breaks

behind them into grass. Fawn gray, or dirt
brown I'd call them, long freakish ears and huge
unfolded tails. They're poised as if

interrupted in mid-thought, gazing
at the still car, at me. These creatures remind
me of my own quiet childhood, the china

animals I played with, gently, their shoe-
box home marked "fragile." Fuzz
on porcelain, thin, gray, the same

color as these rabbits, deer, brush.
The pupils of their brown glass eyes seemed real
until now, when I see these rabbits' eyes

redden, like glass in a kiln. But
these things without motion are living,
posed, proving I cannot drive an inch

farther. Their paws block the road. I pause,
then cut the wheel left to back down
the way I came. But the animals line up

close to the road, so I turn right. Under
my right rear tire I hear something.
I can't tell whether it's china or bone.

The pallor and size of the optic disk indicate current or past damage. The ophthalmologist or neurologist can only see the optic nerve through an MRI or, with the aid of an ophthalmoscope, from the front, where it displays itself as a disk. Imagine a stack of plates. From the side, the pile might resemble a long tube. But if you're looking down on the stack from a great height, it just looks like one plate. Any part could chip and you'd barely notice. I do not know how long it is. What chipped or when.

Retrobulbar

as though the lesion somewhere behind the bulb—
          optic nerve, optic chiasm, orbit
               of fluid under bone—was a pearl
rolling its weight behind and above my eye,
          there in the socket.
                     Whenever I turn my gaze
    it rolls and shifts, digs a little hole.

        Clouds before that eye, swirl and haze.

I imagine it furious and beautiful, nesting there behind the eye.

        May my brown iris
           be replaced by milky pearl.
       (*Those are pearls that were his eyes*)
Staring into the glass I prod the orbit,
          pry open the lids. Where is the stone?
    What must I remove to find it?

On the day we dissected kidneys, Marnie brought her camera. The dissection trays, dull, metal frames with a black, waxy substance lining the inner surface, had accumulated, in their years of use in Dr. Dock's lab, the scent of stale formaldehyde that oozed from every pin-hole in their unruly constellations. I don't recall watching the knife split the kidney. *I will be closing my windows for the night, lowering the blinds, when the impulse to urinate will grip me so suddenly that I refuse to believe its urgency. I will move to the next window. I will pull the sash down, slide the brass lock into place.* What I remember: faint smell of urine mingled with formaldehyde that released to the blade. Impressive to think that despite the preparations the organ distributor had gone to—draining of fluid, injection of dyes—the olfactory evidence of the kidney's work in life lingered and fought scientific inquiry.

I will click the cord to lower the blind. I will twirl the plastic rod to flatten the slats. I will tighten. With our forceps we arranged the halves of the kidney in a composition that attempted to balance the organ's uneven shape, fleshy yin-yang. *I will not run to the toilet; I will hobble, arms swimming through air, as if that could make me faster.* Marnie carried the tray to the lab-room's door. She looked back over her shoulder: "Come on, let's pick some daisies."

We laid the daisies alongside the kidney halves, making sure the stems and angles of the petals complemented the kidney's main arcs. *I will unravel the paper to dry my legs. I will remove my wetted pants and shower. I will wash my clothes.* Within the kidney itself: a tight, red wheel with petal-shaped spokes, almost floral. Marnie removed the lens cap from her Olympus, adjusted the focus. Still life.

The Merle

and then it was my turn to look after
the dog. A blue merle on the barn floor,
one of those cattle herding dogs
from another ranch, come to our farm
to die. *We don't want you; this is not
heaven,* I told the dog. *Go back home.*
She slowly rolled sideways to show her pink
belly, a bright underside slit up
the center, ravaged by maggots. Pearls,
the gaudy kind, adorning the living.

Undressing
the Tree

My father and I undress the oak I will
marry under come summer. *Pulling off
dead wood*, he says. *All that moss strangles
the branches, makes life stagnate . . .*
                                        I pick
a veil of moss from a low branch, steady
it onto my head, silly crown when he's not
looking. It sticks well, tough lace, bundled
knit patches that cling to limb or hair.
                                        What is
beautiful is known to stifle. Like a wildfire
in the pasture, leaping from sage to sage.
Even that couldn't kill this oak, only lick
the bark. I tell my father I'd like
                        some moss
remaining, veiling the air. *But it binds. You
want this tree to be full next year?* Response:
I stoop to collect each scrap from the ground:
the tulle of my own gown and green veil.

The Shaking

I know I scared you last night by shaking,
the only time you were forced to share
a dream that shook me to waking.

Your left hand pressed upon my aching
thigh as it kicked and flailed; how compare
your strength to synapse whims, wild shaking?

You know my nervous system could be taking
over any time; disease is unfair.
Remember: it seems bad when you're waking.

Many times I've trembled when you're making
love to me, my round shoulders open, bare,
but never have I broken into such shaking,

when my body shows us our lives breaking
apart. Still, you hold me. Your kind is rare,
who know (or pretend) dreams seem worse upon waking.

Surprising you stayed: here you are, forsaking
quiet nights for me. Will you be there
when it worsens, my gait palsied with shaking?
Who could be strong enough to hold back its waking?

Heron

The neighbors say it eats their koi fish in the morning, but that's before
I wake up. And though the neighbors are good ones, honest wavers

who stop by now and then, that blue heron never once revealed an orange
mottled slithery thing from the side of its beak, to me, at least. I can't

help but believe that this long neck, a thin alphabet of feathers and muscle,
could hold only the most delicate foods, spiny oat plumes and the tips of
        leaves.

Can't help my marvel at its malleable shape—from zed to dash—and its
        defiant gravity:
weight, slow wings, wind resistant legs, and still it flies. When it alights

on the weakest twig topping the oak, its figure an emblem against the sun,
        please don't
tell me what it's hungry for. It will not bend the branch. It will not shake a
        leaf.

Eating the Night

In his sleep
he chews

the air. I hear
his lips part

and close,
his tongue

click, a thin
lick up

my neck, a finger
cold on the window

over this
bed.

and when I dream
again, he be-

comes the drops
on glass, the waxing

bull moon
pulling me

onto its horns,
its shower of lime-

light and stone.

Nicholas Ray
Directs a Poem

Tonight with the ghost of a horse who shared
his name, he enters my bedroom, his eye-
patch, the horse hooves black against the black
room. He wakes me, explaining the poetry
of the celluloid strip, the magic of the screen.

There is no screen here, only vinyl
window shades. Ray runs his reel humming
from the ceiling fan, lights up the room
with pictures, his life spanning three tall
windows, ten-foot gray walls. All his films,

there in patches—then black-and-white convert
to color, to Natalie Wood's rouged
lips, the red coat Dean gives Sal Mineo,
CinemaScope stretched over folds
and creases, thin Dean hiding in crevices

between window and wall, but I want to
see it all, behind the camera, and below:
the horse's nostril, steam rising
from his sorrel dorsal stripe, the director,
his filmstrip, memory. It all comes

at once, like a kiss in a movie theater,
actually not a theater, more like
a classroom with a stage and screen
in Los Angeles, the memory
of a kiss after the film class when a boy

led me onstage beneath the ten-foot screen,
pushed me into its curtains, quickly read
my face, his rough hands brushing velvet
over my cheeks, and kissed me soft. Every-
thing went red then, the theater a movie

just for us: red seats, walls, screen-kisses,
the light of the projector above us, shining
down a blue ray, flapping the reel's end.
How real memory feels, almost present
like tonight when you, who slept through it all,

roll close, reach for my face like a film star,
kiss me in your dream. Awake, I imagine
Nick the horse, the boy in the theater, James Dean.
If I draw the blanket up high enough,
what is possible beneath such curtains?

I asked Harold if I could see the MRIs. He removed the triangular
wedge under my knees, pulled up the blanket, helped me to
his station behind the frame of glass. Next to a picture of his
grandchild, a large screen monitor. He cycled through a menu of
names. "This one's a stroke." He pointed out a dark spot on the
right hemisphere of another patient's brain. "You see, that's the
blood clot. Laurie, do you believe in God?"
"Yes."
"Good. You should. Because these blood vessels—these here,"
he pointed at some lines in the patient's frontal lobe, "they form
before the bone does. So the bone grows around the veins, and the
brain can be nourished." He seemed mesmerized, as though this
were a recent discovery of something he had been aware of for a
long time, but hadn't, until now, fully examined. "We're just such
miraculous creatures."

Harold pulled up my images. First, the brain: unmistakably my
nose—a little long, funny angle—attached to this brain, which
looked like any brain. Harold showed me the profile, the high
angle view, and finally, what one would see if I were decapitated:
a slice clean through the cervical spine with the underparts of the
brain above. Then he pulled up my orbital scans, the ones focusing
on my eyes, high angle view. I saw the optic nerves and where they
led: short, angled paths toward the center of the brain. My eyes:
globes protruding from the forehead. Harold multiplied the image.
Grayscale Warhol gas mask. Later, on the phone, Mark said all MRI
images end up looking like bad weather. It's bad weather in a gas
mask.

Back Lot
Field Notes

Santa Ynez, California,
El Niño Year

One step and the grass bends, four-foot
arms reaching from earth, swooning like silent
film stars playing the lover spurned. Blades
so untouched they're tinged with artifice,
unnatural. Today they remain moist, soft,
pliable sinews. Come summer each will
bend utterly, strict elbows crooked mid-stalk,
loosening their seed baskets upon the hills—
too real. This is when they become weeds.

•

Branches throw shade mazes across the road,
some sweeping toward you, some curling inward,
labyrinthine. Branch and shadow merge, one path
twisting. The white oaks are what remain after storms.
Leafless, they hold long after evergreens
uproot, snap, fall over, sink in abundance.
Each fold in the oak's gnarled hide is testament:
this is what lasts, this patience, this girth.

•

What keeps you from the sea: a wall of green
mountains, fingers planted, pointing up—the wish
of the ocean. On the other side,
the Figueroas, north and east. Tonight

they will blush despite the lush green where you stand
and behind you. Pink, emblazoned pink
in runnels down the mountainside, too bright
to believe, but last night's sunset offered
proof. You will walk out a door and witness.

Washing Up

Isle of Sheppey, England

What vague assurance brought me here to you in a yellow kitchen?
Praise to holding this invisible envelope—knowing it rests, a rein,

between my ring finger and my last. Praise to failing
memory's insistence that I always walked this way, forgetting

—was it last month?—that I shuffled, propelled the body with a cane;
and to the body's memory, noting what it is to step when I am well.

Praise to forgetting illness swims the channels of my body,
macrophages dining on neurons in my brain; to the daily

ritual of vials and wipes and syringes and needles and ice,
because at least something is being done by science.

Praise to the unused cane I brought; may it rest in its corner of your
    bedroom.
Praise to your parents, to Val, who told me to use the cane if something

goes wrong with the injection, but to pound the floor with it, since neither
she nor Den will hear my voice (BBC2 so loud downstairs—Den, a little
    deaf).

And praise to each needle I break in the machine they gave me.
To a good chill off the Channel, its wreaths of cold circling my legs

when we walked the field today. And to our claim on that field,
because this morning was dry and bright, and because you proposed to me

there before an audience of horses. Praise to the sorrel who shyly
   approached,
who had no interest in the grass we fed him, but stood, open-lipped,

as I let the strands hang from his mouth, the sod at their base releasing
particles against his wooly coat. Praise to the oil and dirt that caked our
   palms

from stroking his nose and neck. Praise to the small, ugly leaf that fell
on my shoulder. I slipped it into my pocket. I remember its weight

tonight, in this unheated yellow kitchen. Praise to the plug in the sink,
to hot water and Fairy Liquid, to not breaking a dish.

Praise to light on foam, to refraction when my wrist dips below the surface.
And praise to you. Your fingers work the towel across my wet hands.

Notes

"Large Loop Excision of the Temporal Zone": The words of American painter Georgia O'Keeffe (1887–1986) appear in italics.

"In Japan, Woman Can Doze with Man Pillow": The italicized lines are quoted from an Associated Press article in which they appear.

"Into Wind": Some phrases come directly from Emily Dickinson's poem 372 ("After great pain, a formal feeling comes").

"Case History: Frankenstein's Lesions": Lines are quoted from James Whale's *Frankenstein* (1931) and Mel Brooks's *Young Frankenstein* (1974). L'hermitte's Sign, a common MS symptom, is characterized by a sudden, electric shock–like sensation pulsing through the body when the patient flexes her head forward. It was first described by Jacques-Jean L'hermitte (1877–1959).

Laurie Clements Lambeth
grew up in southern
California. She received both
MFA and Ph.D. degrees from
the University of Houston.
Her poetry and prose have
been published in such
magazines as the *Paris Review,*
Mid-American Review, Indiana
Review, Iowa Review, and
Alaska Quarterly Review.
She lives in Houston, Texas.
This is her first book.

Rough Cut
Thomas Swiss (1997)

Paris
Jim Barnes (1997)

The Ways We Touch
Miller Williams (1997)

The Rooster Mask
Henry Hart (1998)

The Trouble-Making Finch
Len Roberts (1998)

Grazing
Ira Sadoff (1998)

Turn Thanks
Lorna Goodison (1999)

Traveling Light:
Collected and New Poems
David Wagoner (1999)

Some Jazz a While:
Collected Poems
Miller Williams (1999)

The Iron City
John Bensko (2000)

Songlines in Michaeltree: New and
Collected Poems
Michael S. Harper (2000)

Pursuit of a Wound
Sydney Lea (2000)

The Pebble: Old and New Poems
Mairi MacInnes (2000)

Chance Ransom
Kevin Stein (2000)

House of Poured-Out Waters
Jane Mead (2001)

The Silent Singer: New and
Selected Poems
Len Roberts (2001)

The Salt Hour
J. P. White (2001)

Guide to the Blue Tongue
Virgil Suárez (2002)

The House of Song
David Wagoner (2002)

X =
Stephen Berg (2002)

Arts of a Cold Sun
G. E. Murray (2003)

Barter
Ira Sadoff (2003)

The Hollow Log Lounge
R. T. Smith (2003)

In the Black Window: New and
Selected Poems
Michael Van Walleghen (2004)

A Deed to the Light
Jeanne Murray Walker (2004)

Controlling the Silver
Lorna Goodison (2005)

Good Morning and Good Night
David Wagoner (2005)

American Ghost Roses
Kevin Stein (2005)

Battles and Lullabies
Richard Michelson (2005)

Visiting Picasso
Jim Barnes (2006)

The Disappearing Trick
Len Roberts (2006)

Sleeping with the Moon
Colleen J. McElroy (2007)

Expectation Days
Sandra McPherson (2007)

Tongue & Groove
Stephen Cramer (2007)

National Poetry Series

Eroding Witness
Nathaniel Mackey (1985)
Selected by Michael S. Harper

Palladium
Alice Fulton (1986)
Selected by Mark Strand

Cities in Motion
Sylvia Moss (1987)
Selected by Derek Walcott

The Hand of God and a Few
Bright Flowers
William Olsen (1988)
Selected by David Wagoner

The Great Bird of Love
Paul Zimmer (1989)
Selected by William Stafford

Stubborn
Roland Flint (1990)
Selected by Dave Smith

The Surface
Laura Mullen (1991)
Selected by C. K. Williams

The Dig
Lynn Emanuel (1992)
Selected by Gerald Stern

My Alexandria
Mark Doty (1993)
Selected by Philip Levine

The High Road to Taos
Martin Edmunds (1994)
Selected by Donald Hall

Theater of Animals
Samn Stockwell (1995)
Selected by Louise Glück

The Broken World
Marcus Cafagña (1996)
Selected by Yusef Komunyakaa

Nine Skies
A. V. Christie (1997)
Selected by Sandra McPherson

Lost Wax
Heather Ramsdell (1998)
Selected by James Tate

So Often the Pitcher Goes to Water
until It Breaks
Rigoberto González (1999)
Selected by Ai

Renunciation
Corey Marks (2000)
Selected by Philip Levine

Manderley
Rebecca Wolff (2001)
Selected by Robert Pinsky

Theory of Devolution
David Groff (2002)
Selected by Mark Doty

The University of Illinois Press
is a founding member of the
Association of American University Presses.

Composed in 10/14 Berkeley Old Style
with Frutiger Light display
by Jim Proefrock
at the University of Illinois Press
Designed by Dennis Roberts
Manufactured by Cushing-Malloy, Inc.

University of Illinois Press
1325 South Oak Street
Champaign, IL 61820-6903
www.press.uillinois.edu